CRAZY

CHOICES

FOR
YEAR
OLDS

6

A serious talk about (under)pants

Crazy Choices are designed to bamboozle – but some children may be more bamboozled than others. Bathing suit or swimming costume? Washroom or toilet? There's more: sandwiched between the paleontology and particle physics you'll also find the occasional poo(p), strategic bogey booger and even a mission-critical bum butt or two. I've mixed and matched to keep everyone happy, I hope – but some choices, words and spelling may lead to a little extra head-scratching!

There's only one thing for it: embrace the bum! Savour the humour, and don't tell your head teacher (or mom).
oops **principal**

Design: Fanni Williams / thehappycolourstudio.com
www.matwaugh.co.uk

Produced by Big Red Button Books,
a division of Say So Media Ltd.

ISBN: 978-1-915154-21-7

Published: October 2022
Updated: March 2023

CRAZY CHOICES

Thank you for buying this book. 100% profit goes to children's charities. To find out more, visit matwaugh.co.uk/charity

MAT WAUGH
ILLUSTRATIONS BY YURKO RYMAR

How to play
Crazy Choices

A book you can PLAY?
What will they think of next?

 One-player mode

Take book. Read book. Laugh, read bits to your grandpa or cat and say, "Eurgh, that's disgusting!" Test yourself with the Tricky Trivia questions. Finish book. Send winning lottery ticket to me, the author (optional, highly recommended).

 Two-player mode

Grab a friend and a pen and dive into Brainy's Tricky Trivia starting on page 8. For each question, discuss and make your choice: the same or different, you decide!

Each option has a score, depending on whether it's a brainwave or a truly terrible plan. Turn the page to find out who chose the winner and who picked the stinker. Now add your points to the scorecard on page 113. Who's Yoda, and who's useless?

You're all set. Now go crazy!

Mat

MAKE A CRAZY CHOICE!

Cross the ocean on a dolphin...

OR

...on a shark?

Be too hot...

OR

...too cold?

MAKE A CRAZY CHOICE!

Live alone **OR** live with your whole class?

Have a robot to brush your teeth **OR** a dog to make your breakfast?

Work in a cake shop **OR** a milkshake bar?

Swap brains with an ostrich **OR** swap eyes?

P10

Get squashed by a cloud **OR** a jumbo jet?

P11

Hum while holding your nose **OR** lick your elbow?

P10

Get an itchy nose on a spacewalk...

OR

...have a sneezing fit?

see page 12

BRAIN vs EYES

Did you pick eyes? You're going to look very silly on the class photo: an ostrich's eyes are **massive.**

Each eyeball is bigger than a golf ball... and bigger than its brain! They can see about two miles. But don't let an ostrich hear you say rude things about their walnut-sized brain. They can kick hard enough to kill a lion, and then run away at 40 miles per hour on their long skinny legs.

Brain 2 pts **Eyes** 5 pts

Who cares what you look like when you can see two miles!

HUM vs LICK

Trick question — they're both impossible!

Hum (-4 pts) **Lick** (-4 pts)

This is one you definitely CAN try at home!

CLOUD vs JUMBO JET

Did you choose the **JUMBO JET?** That's the lightest object, so you definitely won't get squashed! Clouds weigh about 500,000 kilograms. That's more than a whopping jumbo jet, even if your mum brings her biggest suitcase. You've won!

Hang on, a scientist is calling. I'll be back in 2 mins.

"WHAT DO YOU WANT, I'M BUSY. REALLY? ARE YOU SURE? OK. I'LL TELL THEM."

So I made a ₜᵢₙy mistake. A cloud won't squash you — but an airplane falling on your head would leave you flatter than a pilot's pancake. That's because the air under clouds is even heavier, so large clouds float on top — but a chunky plane falls through. Ouch!

Cloud `3pts` **Jumbo Jet** `-3pts`

Don't think about it for long or your brain might explode.

ITCH vs SNEEZE

Have you ever been on your bike and suddenly you get an itchy nose? Or perhaps you need to sneeze? What do you do? Maybe you can ride with one hand and use the other to give your schnozz a good scratch. But what if you're cycling in space?

Don't take off your helmet!

Because then you'd be **DEAD.**

For itches, some astronauts stick a bit of stretchy Velcro inside their space helmet. And then, with a twist of the neck, they can give their hooter a good rub. **AAAH,** that's better.

And for sneezes? All you can do, said one astronaut, is "aim low", and hope the snot doesn't spray all over your visor.

Itch `2pts` **Sneeze** `4pts`

Sneezes are messy, but itches are so annoying!

MAKE A CRAZY CHOICE!

Be like a spider, with eight eyes...

It's true – most spiders have eight eyes! It helps them to catch their prey.

OR

...eight legs?

Wake up and believe that you're French* **OR** wake up and think that you're 80 years old?

*Unless you already are French – if so, make it Chinese!

See what a dog sees for a day **OR** a cat?

Rip your trousers when bending over **OR** drop your favourite toy down the toilet?

MAKE A CRAZY CHOICE!

Wake up with the nose of a pig...

...the ears of a donkey?

Clap to clean your teeth...

...clap to flush the toilet?

MAKE A CRAZY CHOICE!

Be super sporty **OR** super brainy

I bet you're both – but you can only choose one!

Keep a tiger as a pet **OR** raise a pack of wolves?

Tidy your bedroom **OR** clean the toilet?

MAKE A CRAZY CHOICE!

Play 'Duck, Duck, Goose!' with a real duck and goose **OR** play 'What's the Time, Mr Wolf?' with a real wolf?

Stub your toe every day **OR** get stung by a nettle instead?

Have super-flat hands **OR** super-flat feet?

MAKE A CRAZY CHOICE!

Have the power to make things smaller...

OR

...make things bigger?

MAKE A CRAZY CHOICE!

Do sums with a box of adders...

2 + 1 =
2 + 2 =
2 + 3 =
2 + 4 =

OR

...share a milkshake with a mamba?

MAKE A CRAZY CHOICE!

Have nine sisters **OR** nine brothers?

Write faster **OR** draw better?

Burp whenever you say hello **OR** blink ten times whenever you say thank you?

Have a million dollars or pounds to spend in one visit to the supermarket  **OR** **to spend at the zoo?**

Wear stinky shoes  **OR** **wear soggy shoes?**

Be the fastest runner in school  **OR** **the best artist?**

MAKE A CRAZY CHOICE!

Be pooped on by a puma...

...peed on by a parrot?

BRAINY'S TRICKY TRIVIA!

Sneak a T-Rex onto the bus without anyone noticing...

OR

...a blue whale?

see page 26

CRAZY CHOICES FOR **6** YEAR OLDS

BRAINY'S TRICKY TRIVIA!

Suck your toe when you're sad **suck your nose?**

 P27

Eat a lump of stinky blue cheese before bedtime **a dandelion salad?**

 P28

Get ignored by your friend **get a cold shoulder?**

 P29

T-REX vs WHALE

How big is a BIG animal? You know that whales are big. You also know that Tyrannosaurus Rex were big ('Rex' means king in Latin, so there's a clue!). And you know that if you took a T-Rex on the bus, it would probably eat the other passengers. And then you.

But in my head — and maybe yours — a blue whale is long and fat. But a T-Rex is **SKY HIGH** - right?

It's time to **RESIZE YOUR MIND.** Because a blue whale is more than twice the height, double the length and **30 TIMES HEAVIER.** It's over twice as long as the bus, too. You might need to open the back window!

T-Rex 2pts **Blue Whale** 7pts

Leave your T-Rex at home - he'll only scare the grannies.

TOE vs NOSE

Some babies suck their **thumbs** when they need cheering up. This is normal. Some people bite

their **toenails** when they're watching TV. This is **DISGUSTING**. What would **YOU** do if nobody was around for a cuddle?

Elephants don't suck their toes; they're just not that **bendy**. But if you say something rude to an elephant, it's quite possible she'll hide away and suck her nose. And as everybody **NOSE**, their **KNOWS** is their trunk. (Oh no, I think I've got my noses confused. I always pick the wrong one!)

Toe (-2 pts) Nose **3 pts**

Tell-tale signs of a toe sucker include wet socks and cheesy breath. I won't let them in the house.

CHEESE vs DANDELION

People say that if you **EAT CHEESE AT BEDTIME**, you'll **HAVE WEIRD DREAMS**. Is it true? Try it and see!

But if you don't like cheese, pick a *dandelion salad*. Did you know that these yellow flowers are edible? And did you also know that the word dandelion come from the Latin? It means **LION'S TEETH** because the leaves are zig-zagged, like teeth. It's like a poem, isn't it? Beautiful.

Another thing you should know: in French, the word for dandelion means *WET THE BED*. They might be tasty, but there's a chance you will have a soggy accident in the night!

Cheese `4 pts` **Dandelion** `-4 pts`

Funny dreams are better than wet sheets: eat the cheese!

Bad luck: it was a **TRICK QUESTION!**

A long time ago, if someone gave you the cold shoulder, they were offering you something to eat — a slice of cold mutton (lamb). Hmm, cold meat: is that all? No roast chicken? No juicy steak or even a few crispy fries? Did you upset them?

And that's what if means if someone gives you **THE COLD SHOULDER** now. Someone is being unfriendly, or ignoring you. So if you chose to be ignored, you were **ALSO** choosing to get the cold shoulder! We call this an **IDIOM**: words with one meaning that we now use to mean something else.

Ignored (-5 pts)   **Cold Shoulder** (-5 pts)

Hungry or ignored: they're both as bad as each other!

**Be given a small
present every week...**

OR

**...a few big
presents
on your
birthday?**

MAKE A CRAZY CHOICE!

Live without sugar **OR** live without salt?

Balance a spoon on your nose **OR** climb 100 steps in 60 seconds?

There's only one way to find out!

Go to clown school **OR** acrobat school?

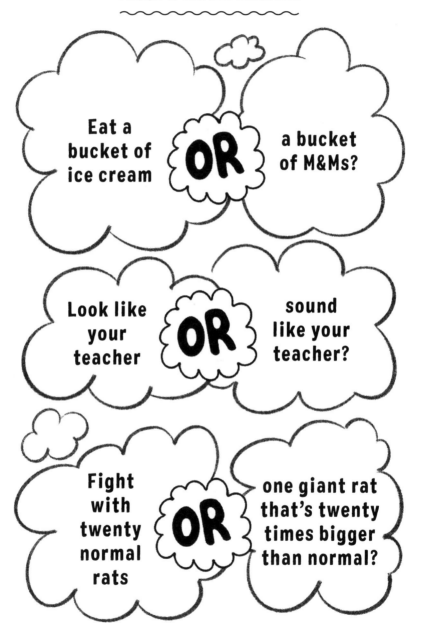

Eat a bucket of ice cream **OR** a bucket of M&Ms?

Look like your teacher **OR** sound like your teacher?

Fight with twenty normal rats **OR** one giant rat that's twenty times bigger than normal?

MAKE A CRAZY CHOICE!

Count the wrinkles on an elephant...

...put a baked bean on every spine of a hedgehog?

MAKE A CRAZY CHOICE!

Do all your own cooking...

...wash all your own clothes?

MAKE A CRAZY CHOICE!

Fight with a ferret **OR** battle with a badger?

Forget how to read **OR** forget how to talk?

Whisper for a day **OR** shout?

MAKE A CRAZY CHOICE!

Walk on tiptoes for a week like a ballet dancer **OR** crawl on your hands and knees for a day, barking like a dog?

Spend a night with Father Christmas **OR** the tooth fairy?

Never lose anything ever again **OR** be able to find things that other people have lost?

MAKE A CRAZY CHOICE!

Have the biggest feet in the world...

...the smallest?

BRAINY'S TRICKY TRIVIA!

Race a sneeze...

see page 40

OR

...race a cheetah?

BRAINY'S TRICKY TRIVIA!

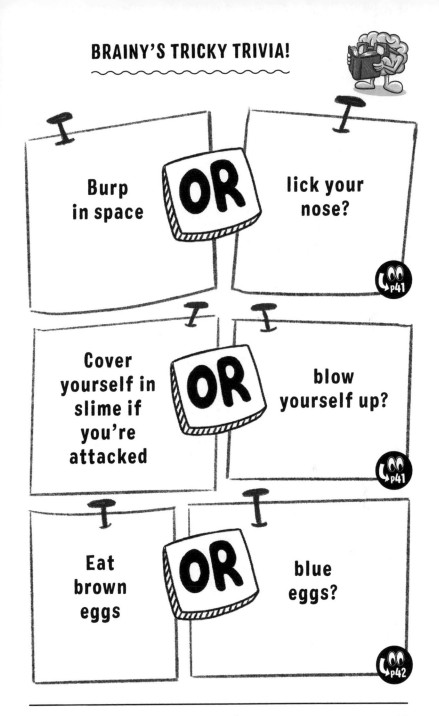

Burp in space **OR** lick your nose?

p41

Cover yourself in slime if you're attacked **OR** blow yourself up?

p41

Eat brown eggs **OR** blue eggs?

p42

SNEEZE vs CHEETAH

Imagine. You and a cheetah line up, ready to race. Suddenly, an antelope runs past with a pepper

pot. You sneeze (no hands — ugh!). The gun fires: the sneeze and the cheetah are OFF! Who will win? Let's find out!

"There they go! With three bounds, that cheetah is already running at 60mph — amazing! But look — the spray from that grubby child's mouth is shooting out at 100mph!

Wait! The spit is slowing down... a cloud of germs is settling on the track, 9 metres away. But the cheetah is around the bend and out of sight!"

IT'S A WIN FOR THE CHEETAH
(BUT THE ANTELOPE IS IN TROUBLE!)

Sneeze `6pts` **Cheetah** `4pts`

For speed, pick the sneeze. But cheetahs run farther!

BURP vs LICK

If you chose burp, bad luck! You'll be **SICK** instead. **IT'S IMPOSSIBLE TO BURP IN SPACE.** But about one in twenty people can lick their nose. So even if you can't, someone in your class probably can!

Burp (−5 pts) **Nose** **1pt**

Grab an extra 5 points if you can roll your tongue, too!

SLIME vs EXPLODE

To live a long life, get slimy. That's what the hagfish does when it is attacked. Sharks spit them out. Prefer explosions? When termites in South America are attacked, old worker termites march out and blow themselves up, spraying the enemy with poison and saving the younger termites. Yay!

Slime **9 pts** **Explode** **5 pts**

Explode once or be slimy for life? Slime wins!

BROWN vs BLUE

We're talking about the colour of the shell, not the inside! (If you ever crack an egg and it's blue or brown inside... run away.)

In the USA, shoppers usually buy white eggs. Brown eggs are more common in the UK. But eggs can also be blue, or green. What colour eggs do you eat? They all taste the same, so choose eggs to match your egg cup!

Different breeds of chicken lay different colours. Look at their tiny earlobes for a clue. Dark earlobes = brown eggs. White earlobes = white. Blue earlobes = err, blue. And red and yellow spotty earlobes with a bow tie mean you're looking at a chicken dressed up as a clown.

Brown `3 pts` **Blue** `3 pts`

Pick any colour you like, they all taste delicious on toast!

MAKE A CRAZY CHOICE!

Blink to make vegetables disappear...

...make your teacher vanish instead?

MAKE A CRAZY CHOICE!

Keep a secret squirrel in your hair...

...a hamster hidden in your pocket?

MAKE A CRAZY CHOICE!

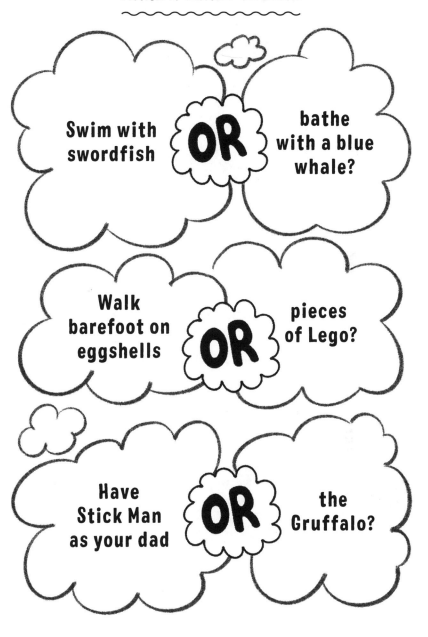

Swim with swordfish **OR** bathe with a blue whale?

Walk barefoot on eggshells **OR** pieces of Lego?

Have Stick Man as your dad **OR** the Gruffalo?

MAKE A CRAZY CHOICE!

Eat a doughnut without licking your lips  **OR** **without using your hands?**

Learn how to juggle  **OR** **walk on stilts?**

Fight fires  **OR** **chase criminals?**

MAKE A CRAZY CHOICE!

Break your leg...

...break your arm?

MAKE A CRAZY CHOICE!

Have tea with a T-Rex...

OR

...dinner with a diplodocus?

MAKE A CRAZY CHOICE!

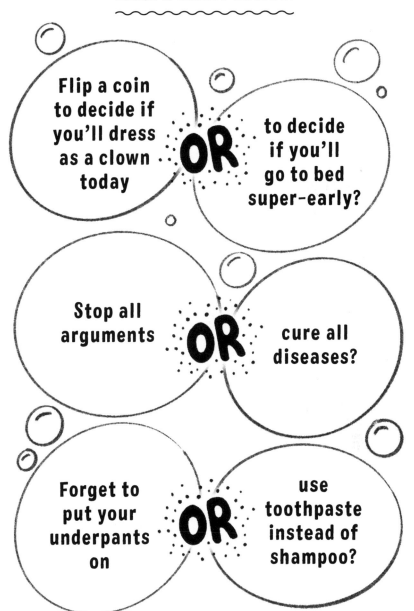

Flip a coin to decide if you'll dress as a clown today **OR** to decide if you'll go to bed super-early?

Stop all arguments **OR** cure all diseases?

Forget to put your underpants on **OR** use toothpaste instead of shampoo?

MAKE A CRAZY CHOICE!

Share a space rocket with a monkey **OR** a kangaroo?

Know the words to every song **OR** the moves to every dance?

Wake up on a desert island **OR** in space?

MAKE A CRAZY CHOICE!

Get a job as a chicken tickler...

OR

...teaching goats to play football?

BRAINY'S TRICKY TRIVIA!

Paint your cows with stripes like a zebra...

OR

...with spots like a leopard?

see page
54

CRAZY CHOICES FOR **6** YEAR OLDS

BRAINY'S TRICKY TRIVIA!

Talk with an elephant **OR** chat with Alex, an African grey parrot? P56

Have a long bath with bubbles **OR** with a bath bomb? P57

Put toothpaste back in the tube **OR** milk a whale? P57

STRIPES vs SPOTS

...ten marked by farmers, usually to

...wns them. Flocks of sheep have also been

DYED DIFFERENT COLOURS for TV adverts. But why

would you paint stripes on your cows? **HOLD ON**

TO YOUR MILKSHAKES because

I'm going to give you TWO

reasons!

FIRST REASON TO PAINT STRIPES ON A COW

During World War II, the United Kingdom turned off
the lights. This was known as the BLACKOUT.
Street lights and car lights were turned off,
and every window had to be covered.
Blackouts made it much harder for German
pilots to **DROP BOMBS,** because they couldn't see
where the cities were. But down on the ground it
made it very hard to drive! And if you met a herd

of BLACK COWS on a BLACK NIGHT, you'd have problems, and so would the cows. Farmers had an answer: paint white stripes on the cows so they

Two cows in a field at night. One is lying down and winking. Do you see the problem?

could be seen more easily! (What happened if a cow stood on a zebra crossing or crosswalk, I wonder?)

SECOND REASON TO PAINT STRIPES ON A COW

Scientists have discovered that cows painted with stripes don't get bitten by flies as much. The stripes confuse the bugs and they fly too fast at the cow and **bounce off,** probably with a headache.

So what happens if you paint a cow with spots? Who knows? I just made that one up to confuse you!

Stripes `10 pts` **Spots** `0 pt`

It's a home run for stripes!

ELEPHANT vs PARROT

They say that elephants never forget. Imagine what they could tell you! Sadly that's impossible, but they can talk to each other. They even have an elephant word that means, *"Humans are coming! Run away!"* Seriously!

So what about Alex, the parrot? Plenty of birds can copy humans and say a few words. But Alex learned over **100 WORDS.** He could count up to six and knew his colours. If he did something bad, he squawked, "I'm sorry." He sometimes gave the wrong answer on purpose. CHEEKY!

Sadly, Alex died a few years ago, aged 31. His last words were the ones he said every night to his owner:

"YOU BE GOOD, I LOVE YOU. SEE YOU TOMORROW."

Elephant (0 pts) **Alex** (0 pts)
Elephants can't talk, and Alex is an ex-parrot. Sorry.

BUBBLES vs BOMB

BATH BOMBS are fun. They fizz like crazy, and turn the water a funny colour. But if you play in the bath until you're as *WRINKLY AS A WALNUT*, then choose the bubbles. They act like a blanket and keep the bath water warm for longer. Just don't pop them!

A picture of you, after a long bath

Bubbles `4 pts` **Bomb** `2 pts`

A cold bath is no fun, whatever colour it is!

TOOTHPASTE vs MILK

I don't know how you'd do either of these. But I can tell you that the jobs aren't as different as you think — because **whale milk** is so thick it's like **TOOTHPASTE**. Why? So it doesn't dissolve before it reaches the baby whale!

Toothpaste `11 pts` **Milk** `11 pts`

If you can do either of these, you deserve the points!

MAKE A CRAZY CHOICE!

Celebrate your birthday every day...

...celebrate Christmas instead?

MAKE A CRAZY CHOICE!

Climb any tree like a monkey  **run as fast as a cheetah?**

Live where everything is white  **everything is black?**

Learn sign language  **use a computer to speak?**

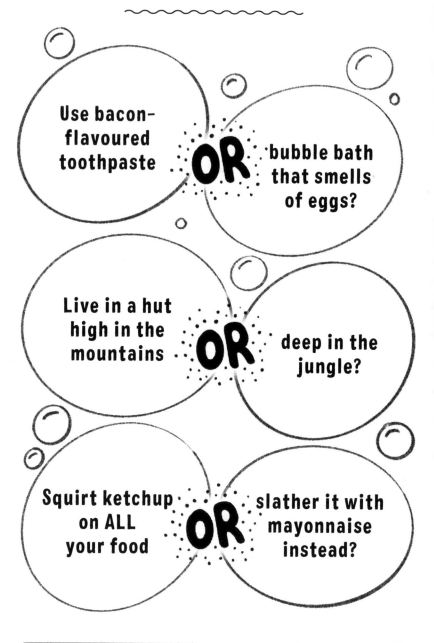

Use bacon-flavoured toothpaste **OR** bubble bath that smells of eggs?

Live in a hut high in the mountains **OR** deep in the jungle?

Squirt ketchup on ALL your food **OR** slather it with mayonnaise instead?

MAKE A CRAZY CHOICE!

Make it snow when you want...

...make it a sunny day?

MAKE A CRAZY CHOICE!

Be given a small bar of chocolate for yourself...

OR

...a large bar to share with your family?

MAKE A CRAZY CHOICE!

Drink a burger smoothie **OR** hot dog soup?

Be afraid of sunlight **OR** be afraid of CAPITAL LETTERS?

Oops: SORRY!

Be a goat **OR** a dog?

MAKE A CRAZY CHOICE!

Be able to run at the speed of light **OR** make yourself invisible?

Find a beanstalk in your garden **OR** a gingerbread house next door?

Climb Mount Everest in your slippy socks **OR** canoe down the Amazon in a sieve?

MAKE A CRAZY CHOICE!

Sleep outside...

...sleep standing up?

Be swallowed
by a snake...

OR

...a whale?

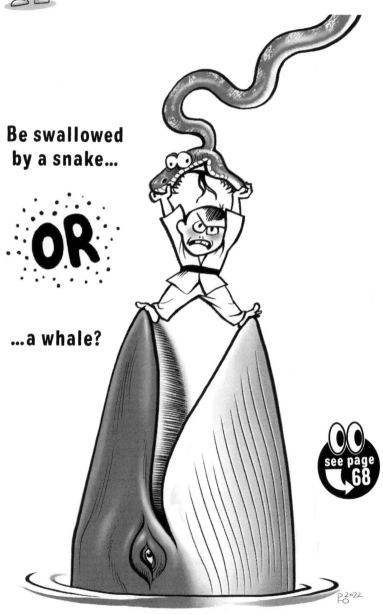

see page 68

Run an egg and spoon race for a marathon (26 miles!)  draw a line on the floor with a pencil until it runs out?

 P69

Hold your breath longer than a sloth  longer than a dolphin?

 P70

Sleep in a coffin  an ice hotel?

 P71

SNAKE vs WHALE

If you've read about **JONAH AND THE WHALE** you might think that you could survive a whale gobble. Is it true?

A man diving for lobster got caught in a humpback whale's mouth, but the whale SPAT HIM OUT (maybe he tasted funny). Only a sperm whale is big enough to swallow a person. They spend most of their life deep under water, so it is **VERY** unlikely to happen.

African rock pythons sometimes swallow crocodiles and antelopes. Could they swallow **YOU?** You're more likely to get hit by a meteorite (BAD), or win the lottery (GOOD) — although these probably won't happen either. Do write and tell me if I'm wrong!

Snake **3pts** Whale **5pts**

Those python fangs could be spiky. Ouch!

MARATHON vs PENCIL

So which is longer: the marathon or the pencil line?

I DON'T KNOW. SORRY NOT SORRY NO REFUNDS.

 We know about the egg and spoon race marathon, because a man called Dale managed it in less than four hours. This is much faster than most people could manage *without* the egg!

But how long would the pencil line be? You'd have to use a sharpener of course, but would it reach the end of the road? To the next town? Nobody knows. Some say 35 miles. Others says that's rubbish: it's maybe eight or nine miles. There's only one way to find out, and when you're finished can you let me know, please?

Marathon `10 pts` **Pencil** `8 pts`
Either way, you'll ache for days!

SLOTH vs DOLPHIN

Is it the obvious answer — the dolphin? or is it the trick answer, the sloth? One of them can manage 20 minutes under water. The other can hold their puff for 40 minutes. But which is which?

The animal to beat is... the sloth! Sloths do everything slowly. They can slow down their heartbeat, which means they can hold their breath for twice as long as a dolphin.

Here's something else they do slowly: **poo.** It takes them a week to get ready. Then they climb down slowly from their tree, walk to their favourite place and do the most enormous poop you can imagine. You can have that fact for free.

Sloth `6 pts` **Dolphin** `1pt`

Dolphin pickers still get a point because they're so cute.

COFFIN vs ICE HOTEL

Why would you choose to sleep in a coffin? When you have no other option. That's what homeless people could do a hundred years ago: stay at a **COFFIN HOUSE,** where for 4p (5c) you could sleep in a dusty coffin. You didn't have to share it with anyone, alive or dead — but you still wouldn't sleep very well.*

Ice hotels are a much more comfy choice. You could go to one today, in Sweden, where they build a new hotel every year. The walls, the roof, even the furniture: it's all made of ice. Don't stay too long, though; anyone who stays until spring will definitely wet the bed!

* Because of all the coffin, of course!

Coffin 10 pts **Ice Hotel** 8 pts

Extra bravery points if you chose the coffin!

MAKE A CRAZY CHOICE!

Be a cat...

...a dog?

MAKE A CRAZY CHOICE!

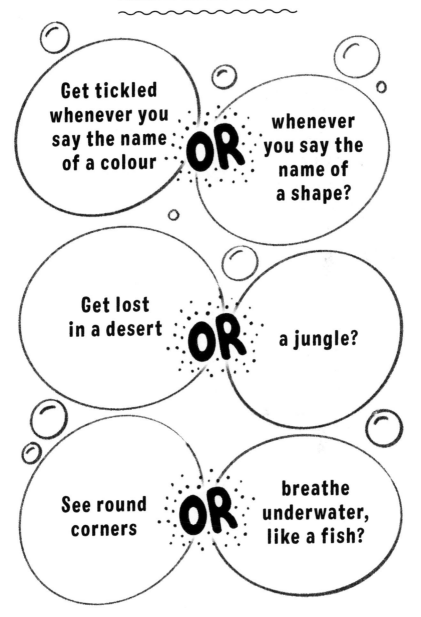

Get tickled whenever you say the name of a colour **OR** whenever you say the name of a shape?

Get lost in a desert **OR** a jungle?

See round corners **OR** breathe underwater, like a fish?

Without help, would you rather try cooking dinner for your family

OR

do the food shopping?

Live in a house designed like a giant bottle

OR

like a woolly mammoth?

Get stuck up a tree like a cat

OR

lock yourself in a wardrobe by mistake?

MAKE A CRAZY CHOICE!

Be the clever clogs
who invented
the wheel...

OR

...the first cave dweller to discover fire?

MAKE A CRAZY CHOICE!

Have a tummy ache...

...a headache?

MAKE A CRAZY CHOICE!

Play football on the moon **OR** play underwater tennis?

Have your own private army **OR** your own private chef?

Have orange teeth **OR** purple teeth?

MAKE A CRAZY CHOICE!

Tidy your room once a day  spend one day a year tidying it?

Count raindrops on a window  count the leaves on a tree?

Use a trampoline to get upstairs  use a slide to get downstairs?

MAKE A CRAZY CHOICE!

Wear spotty clothes...

stripy clothes?

Scratch a gorilla's tummy...

see page 82

OR

...tickle him under the chin?

BRAINY'S TRICKY TRIVIA!

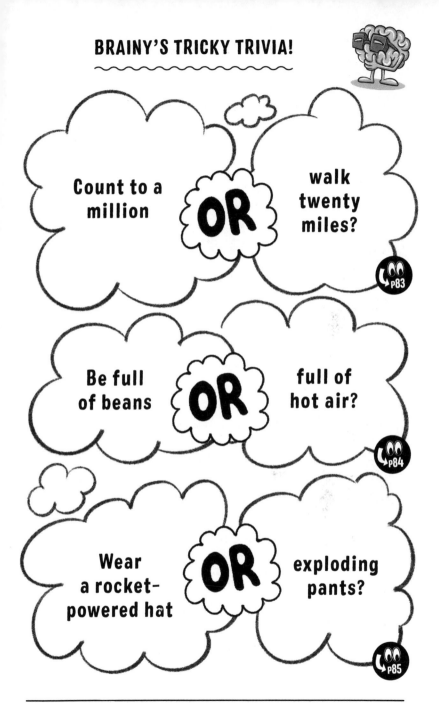

Count to a million **OR** walk twenty miles?

P83

Be full of beans **OR** full of hot air?

P84

Wear a rocket-powered hat **OR** exploding pants?

P85

TUMMY vs CHIN

Both of these sound dangerous, don't they? Would it help you to know that gorillas like to be tickled? No, it wouldn't. Because only THE TUMMY RUB is possible and here's why:

gorillas don't have chins.

Nor do chimps, dogs, cats... or anyone or anything except humans. Eh?

Here's your chinny fact for today. A chin isn't the place where your bottom teeth live: that's your jaw. It's the sticky-out bit underneath that. Give it a feel now. And we're the only animals that have chins... *and nobody knows why.*

My answer? Because if you didn't have a chin, **YOUR BEARD WOULD FALL OFF.** And that's why I'm not a scientist.

Tummy (-2 pts) **Chin** (-8 pts)

Chin is impossible, but a tummy tickle is still a risky move!

COUNT vs WALK

 Walking can get pretty boring. And tiring. And you're good at counting, right? So perhaps you chose that? **WRONG!**

Many children could walk 20 miles in a day. But could you count to a million in a day? No! A week? Still no! What about a month? STILL no!

And how do we know? Because a man called Jeremy did it. He slept a little bit, and ate a little bit, and even went to the toilet. But the rest of the time he counted. All day, every day. And it took him **THREE MONTHS.** To celebrate, he did a little chicken dance. Perhaps all that counting had sent him loopy.

90 DAYS

Walk `2 pts` Count `-2 pts`

A 20 mile walk suddenly seems like a good idea!

BEANS vs HOT AIR

This is a **DOUBLE-IDIOM QUESTION.**

Here's how it works.

IDIOM 1: If you give beans to kids for tea, two things will happen. Firstly, you'll need to open a window. Secondly, they'll be full of energy! Horse owners used to feed them beans so they'd run faster. So if you say someone is FULL OF BEANS, this is a good thing.

IDIOM 2: Bean-eating children are also full of hot (stinky) air. But if you say someone is FULL OF HOT AIR, you're not talking about what they had for lunch. It means they've got lots to say but none of it is very important.

Beans `5pts` **Hot Air** `0pts`

Beans good, hot air bad!

HAT vs TROUSERS

As far as I know, you can't buy a hat with a rocket on it. Probably because it would blow your head off. **This Is Not Good.**

Exploding trousers or pants aren't great for your health, either. But that's what farmers in New Zealand wore around 90 years ago. The trousers weren't meant to explode, but they started going **BANG!** and catching fire after farmers accidentally sprayed themselves with a new weedkiller. **OUCH!**

Hat **1pt** Trousers (–3 pts)

The hat is the safe bet, because it hasn't been invented.

Walk to school in a thunderstorm...

OR

...walk home in one?

MAKE A CRAZY CHOICE!

Coat yourself in peanut butter **OR** honey?

Discover a new country **OR** discover a new planet?

Make grown-ups say yes **OR** say no?

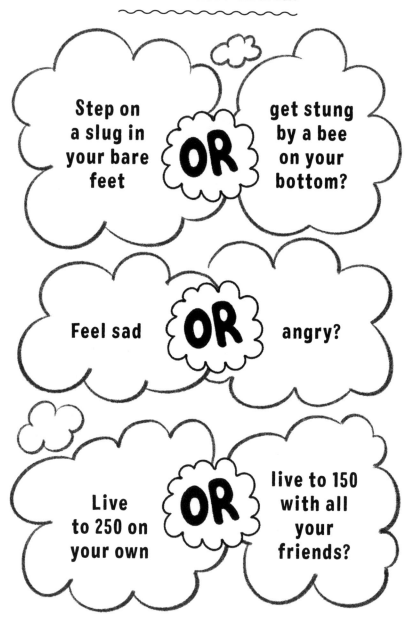

MAKE A CRAZY CHOICE!

Have no knees...

...no elbows?

MAKE A CRAZY CHOICE!

Have a cold bath...

OR

...a cold shower?

MAKE A CRAZY CHOICE!

Find a gold coin under your pillow  **a diamond in your pocket?**

Eat salty doughnuts  **sugary fries?**

Have grey hair  **false teeth?**

MAKE A CRAZY CHOICE!

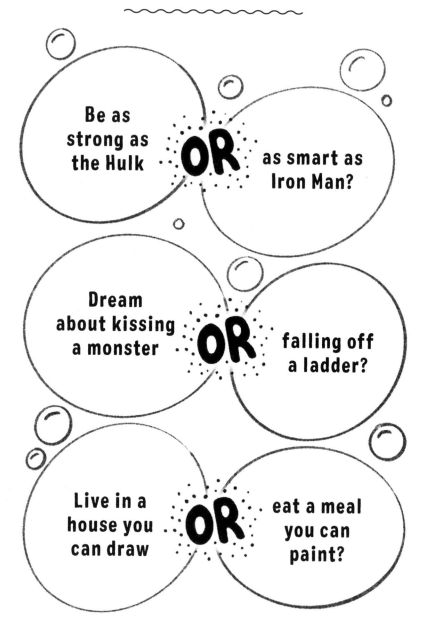

Be as strong as the Hulk **OR** as smart as Iron Man?

Dream about kissing a monster **OR** falling off a ladder?

Live in a house you can draw **OR** eat a meal you can paint?

MAKE A CRAZY CHOICE!

Be clean... **OR** ...be dirty?

MAKE A CRAZY CHOICE!

Have an upside
down nose...

...upside down
ears?

MAKE A CRAZY CHOICE!

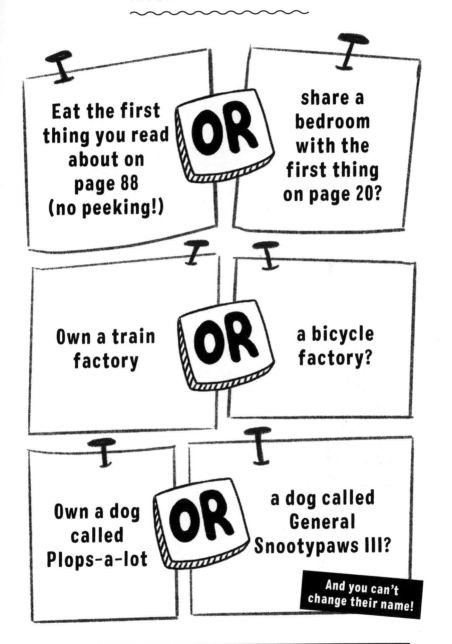

Eat the first thing you read about on page 88 (no peeking!) **OR** share a bedroom with the first thing on page 20?

Own a train factory **OR** a bicycle factory?

Own a dog called Plops-a-lot **OR** a dog called General Snootypaws III?

And you can't change their name!

MAKE A CRAZY CHOICE!

Freeze things like Elsa **OR** be as funny as Anna?

Get ants in your pants **OR** stones in your shoes?

Play dominoes on a roller coaster **OR** do cartwheels in a hot air balloon?

MAKE A CRAZY CHOICE!

Play piano
like Mozart...

OR

...draw like
Leonardo
da Vinci?

BRAINY'S TRICKY TRIVIA!

Eat upside down...

see page 100

OR

...sleep upside down?

BRAINY'S TRICKY TRIVIA!

Own a pet called ARRRRR

 **OR**

a pet called I'm Slippy?

 P101

Both have won prizes. Which would you want in your living room?

Read a story backwards

 **OR**

in the mirror?

 P102

Be over the hill

 **OR**

sit on a fence?

 P101

EAT vs SLEEP

Both are on the **DO NOT TRY THIS AT HOME** list, but only one of these is **deadly**: falling

(If you're a bat, or a sloth, or a manatee, ignore this bit: you already do it.)

asleep upside down. It's dangerous to even try it, because if you stay upside down for too long the blood rushes to your head and can cause a brain injury, or even kill you.

What about eating? Doesn't food fall into your tummy? Not really: food is pushed into your stomach by muscles in your oesophagus — the tube your food goes down. These muscles work even if you're hanging upside down off a hot air balloon. But this activity also goes on my **DO NOT TRY THIS** list because you might choke. And I won't come to rescue you because I don't like heights.

Eat (-2 pts) Sleep (-2 pts)

Two terrible ideas (unless you're a bat).

ARRRR vs I'M SLIPPY

ARRRR was a racehorse that won US$100,000 (£90,000)! **I'M SLIPPY** is a good pick, too: this **GREYHOUND** won lots of races. Nobody could catch him!

ARRRR `5 pts` **I'm Slippy** `5 pts`

Everyone's a winner!

HILL vs FENCE

DOUBLE-IDIOM ALERT! If someone says you're **OVER THE HILL,** it means you're past the middle point of your life, and that you're getting old. I hear it quite a lot. **CHEEKY!**

But if you sit on the fence, it's because you can't decide which side to choose. You'll get a splinter up your bum and it will serve you right.

Hill `-3 pts` **Fence** `1 pt`

At least you get a good view when you sit on a fence.

BACKWARDS vs MIRROR

Could you read a story backwards – starting with the last word, and reading to the first?

Let's give it a go!

!BACKWARDS STORIES READING AND TV PIZZA, LOVED WHO OLD YEAR SIX CLEVER VERY A WAS THERE TIME A UPON ONCE

It's pretty tricky, but I bet you managed it! But what if the words are in the right order, but the letters are backwards? That's called mirror writing, because you can use a mirror to read it. Try holding this book up to see the secret message from your parents!

WHO MADE THAT STINKY SMELL? AND STOP PICKING YOUR NOSE WHEN YOU THINK I'M NOT LOOKING!

Backwards `10 pts` **Mirror** `12 pts`

Big points for these because they're both so hard!

MAKE A CRAZY CHOICE!

Follow...

OR

...lead?

MAKE A CRAZY CHOICE!

Live in a treehouse...

OR

...a secret cave?

MAKE A CRAZY CHOICE!

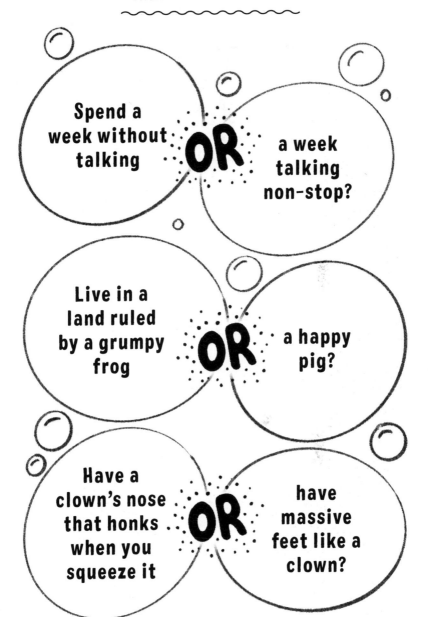

Spend a week without talking **OR** a week talking non-stop?

Live in a land ruled by a grumpy frog **OR** a happy pig?

Have a clown's nose that honks when you squeeze it **OR** have massive feet like a clown?

MAKE A CRAZY CHOICE!

Wear Superman's tights to bed **OR** Batman's cape to school?

Be kind **OR** be generous?

Sit in a bath of worms for an hour **OR** sleep in a cave full of bats?

MAKE A CRAZY CHOICE!

Be chased by an elephant...

OR

...a tiger?

MAKE A CRAZY CHOICE!

Be a tiny explorer inside a beehive...

...inside a snake's nest?

MAKE A CRAZY CHOICE!

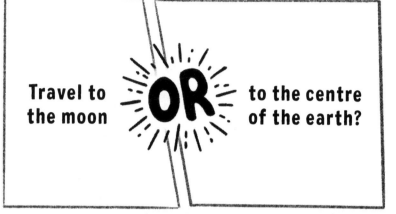

Travel to the moon **OR** **to the centre of the earth?**

Make any photo come to life **OR** **any drawing?**

Have a whisk instead of a right hand **OR** **a mop instead of a left leg?**

MAKE A CRAZY CHOICE!

Dream that your legs are made of jelly...

...your arms are made of sausages?

One Last Crazy Choice!

I hoped you enjoyed making all these crazy choices. And now you also know more about clouds, lonely elephants and space burps. One day, you'll thank me for that.*

Here's your last head scratcher: will you keep this book a secret? Or will you find a way to give your opinion to everyone you know, and millions more you don't? Grown-ups do this all the time – why shouldn't you?

If you have something to say, ask a parent to leave a review wherever they bought this book. (You may need to write it for them – you know what grown-ups are like).

I can't wait to find out what you think!

*When you are flying a spaceship, taking off through heavy cloud while sipping a fizzy drink with your elephant pilot pal Jim Jumbo strapped in alongside you. It'll happen, believe me.

BRAINY'S SCORECARD

Player ❶................. **Player ❷** ....

Page		˅SCORE˅ ❶ ❷		Page		˅SCORE˅ ❶ ❷	
10	Brain vs Eyes			57	Bubbles vs Bomb		
10	Hum vs Lick			57	Toothpaste vs Milk		
11	Cloud vs Jumbo Jet			68	Snake vs Whale		
12	Itch vs Sneeze			69	Marathon vs Pencil		
26	T-Rex vs Whale			70	Sloth vs Dolphin		
27	Toe vs Nose			71	Coffin vs Ice Hotel		
28	Cheese vs Dandelion			82	Tummy vs Chin		
29	Ignored vs Shoulder			83	Count vs Walk		
40	Sneeze vs Cheetah			84	Beans vs Hot Air		
41	Burp vs Lick			85	Hat vs Trousers		
41	Slime vs Explode			100	Eat vs Sleep		
42	Brown vs Blue			101	ARRRRR vs I'm Slippy		
54	Stripes vs Spots			101	Hill vs Fence		
56	Elephant vs Parrot			102	Backwards vs Mirror		
	TOTAL:				GRAND TOTAL:		

My Life of Choices

I've made some terrible choices in my life.

✈ When I was your age, I dribbled modelling glue on the radiator. I planned to peel it off later (very satisfying). But I forgot, and sat in it instead.

🏠 When I was nine, I dropped an epic water balloon from a bedroom window at my friend's house. It fell inside the house, not outside. It was his parents' bedroom.

🏃 When I was sixteen, I skipped breakfast. In assembly I fainted and fell head-first into a row of children three years below me. I can still hear them laughing.

But then I grew up and I started making excellent decisions!

🐘 I decided that an African elephant wasn't flapping its ears to be friendly, and that we should run. Fast.

🎢 I took a trip to a theme park where I met Mrs Waugh. She wasn't called that then, of course. That would be weird.

➕ I did home improvements in flip-flops. Actually, forget that one: I had to visit hospital with a rusty nail sticking out of my foot. The nurses said that it served me right, and that men of my age shouldn't wear flip-flops.

See? I'm super-wise now, and my family agree (they don't).

What's the best and worst decision *you've* ever made? I'd love to hear from you – your parents can email me!

mail@matwaugh.co.uk